the guide to owning a
Scottish Terrier

Muriel Lee

Photo: Paulette Braun

© T.F.H. Publications, Inc.

Distributed in the UNITED STATES to the Pet Trade by T.F.H. Publications, Inc., 1 TFH Plaza, Neptune City, NJ 07753; on the Internet at www.tfh.com; in CANADA by Rolf C. Hagen Inc., 3225 Sartelon St., Montreal, Quebec H4R 1E8; Pet Trade by H & L Pet Supplies Inc., 27 Kingston Crescent, Kitchener, Ontario N2B 2T6; in ENGLAND by T.F.H. Publications, PO Box 74, Havant PO9 5TT; in AUSTRALIA AND THE SOUTH PACIFIC by T.F.H. (Australia), Pty. Ltd., Box 149, Brookvale 2100 N.S.W., Australia; in NEW ZEALAND by Brooklands Aquarium Ltd., 5 McGiven Drive, New Plymouth, RD1 New Zealand; in SOUTH AFRICA by Rolf C. Hagen S.A. (PTY.) LTD., P.O. Box 201199, Durban North 4016, South Africa; in JAPAN by T.F.H. Publications. Published by T.F.H. Publications, Inc.

**MANUFACTURED IN THE
UNITED STATES OF AMERICA
BY T.F.H. PUBLICATIONS, INC.**

Contents

The Publisher wishes to acknowledge the following owners of the dogs in this book: Donna Cone, Sharon Ero, Ann Frankenwich, Glenda Kaplan, Mary Parotti, Ann Schumann, Don and Sharon Sears, Amanda Thomas.

Photo: Paulette Braun

Introduction to the Scottish Terrier

Ah, the Scottish Terrier! The big dog in the little package; the tyke with the short legs and the long head; the dog that has the courage of a German Shepherd and thinks that he is the size of a Great Dane. Perhaps the writer William Haynes said it best: "Words fail me when I want to describe the Scottish Terrier. To me he is the dog of dogs, my personal opinion being: all dogs are good; any terrier is better; a Scottie is best!"

This is not a dog for everyone, but those who have had a Scottish Terrier as a comrade will never forget the experience. For many, Scotties will become lifelong companions, and each Scot in the household that goes to his reward is replaced with a new Scottie puppy. Indeed, once your heart is given to a Scottish Terrier, it will remain true and steadfast to the breed for a lifetime.

The courage and tenacity of the Scottish Terrier makes him the ultimate example of a big dog in a small package. *Photo: Paulette Braun*

History of the Scottish Terrier

In the history of the dog world, the Scottish Terrier is not an ancient breed; however, its official beginnings, which trace back to the late 1800s, place it among one of the older breeds recognized by the American Kennel Club (AKC).

The Scottish Terrier belongs to the group of dogs described as terriers, from the Latin word, *terra*, meaning earth. The terrier is a dog that has been bred to work beneath the ground to drive out small and large vermin, rodents, and other

The Scottie belongs to the Terrier Group and was originally bred to drive out vermin on farms and estates. *Photo: Robert Pearcy*

Almost all of the terrier breeds originated in the British Isles and through crossbreeding derived from similar ancestors. *Photo: Isabelle Francais*

By the late 1800s, the Scottish Terrier was well established in Scotland and began to accumulate admirers in England and the US. *Photo: Tara Darling*

animals that can be a nuisance to country living.

All of the dogs in the terrier group originated in the British Isles, with the exception of the Miniature Schnauzer. Many of the terrier breeds were derived from a similar ancestor, and as recently as the mid-1800s, the terriers fell roughly into two basic categories: the rough-coated, short-legged dogs of Scotland, and the longer-legged, smooth-coated dogs of England.

The family of Scotch Terriers—those bred in Scotland—divide themselves into the modern Scottish Terrier, the West Highland White Terrier, and the Dandie Dinmont Terrier. The Skye Terrier is also considered to be a part of this group. In the early 1800s, dogs that were referred to as the Scotch Terrier could be any of the first three breeds mentioned. Interbreeding was common among these breeds, and all three breed types could come from one litter.

As breeders started exhibiting at dog shows, it was realized that there must be more uniformity within the breed, i.e., all pups in a litter should look alike, as well as being of the same type as their sire and dam.

In 1882, a group of Scottish Terrier fanciers from Scotland met and formed a breed club. Although this club had many difficulties and did not survive, these breeders were able to reach some unanimity and initiated the writing and the acceptance of the first breed standard. By the mid-1890s, some stability as to type was finally brought to the breed. By 1900, the Scottie was a well-established breed with many friends and fanciers in the British Isles. Interest in the United States was developing as a small and dedicated group of friends of the Scottish Terrier was growing on American shores.

The terrier development coincided with the advent of dog shows, and the first dog

THE GUIDE TO OWNING A SCOTTISH TERRIER

As his popularity grew, the Scottie became well known as a formidable show dog and an amicable companion. *Photo: Isabelle Francais*

show to take place in America was in 1874, 15 years after the first dog show in England. The first Scottish Terrier to be exhibited in America was in 1883. In comparison to the sporting breeds, terriers were slow to take hold in popularity in America in the early 1900s, but with the perseverance of several men, the Scottish Terrier was fairly well established by the late 1910s. He was on his way to becoming not only a beloved pet of the general population, but a formidable competitor in the show ring.

English dogs with impressive pedigrees were now imported into America, and it is these dogs, with their strong genetic backgrounds, that made a major contribution to the Scottish Terrier for several decades in America.

By the 1930s, the Scottie was well-known and one of the most popular breeds in America. President Franklin D. Roosevelt had his Scottish Terrier, Fala, who was not only a beloved pet of the president, but a great favorite with the press. Fala was pictured many times sitting with the president or riding in his car. Fala died two days short of his 12th birthday and was buried in the rose garden at Hyde Park, six feet away from his beloved master.

Scottish Terriers have remained a very stable breed, just as their owners are relatively stable and conservative. The breed stays right around 35th in popularity among the AKC recognized breeds and continues to have its admirers.

Watch the Westminster Kennel Club show that is televised for two nights every year in early February. You will see the Scottish Terrier in all of his glory—striding out proudly with his handler, with his smart fur jacket plucked to elegance and glowing in the show lights. He has won Best in Show six times at this crown jewel of dog shows!

Throughout the years, the Scottish Terrier has remained a favorite of dog lovers because of his gregarious nature and devotion to his master. *Photo: Isabelle Francais*

Characteristics of the Scottish Terrier

Scottish Terriers have been described in many ways, and all the names fit the breed: lion-hearted, robust, alert, curious, scrappy, bright-eyed, intelligent, sturdy, courageous, and adaptable. This is a breed with pluck and intelligence. They are sensitive to both

A plucky and intelligent breed, the Scottie is a versatile dog that can participate in almost any activity. *Photo: Isabelle Francais*

criticism and praise. They are adaptable, and if given good food, a bed, and love, they can adjust to almost any living condition with little difficulty. The Scottie is a below-the-knee dog that is long on gameness, determination, and courage—in no way can he be regarded as a Toy dog. It has been said that a Scottie is a dog that "can go anywhere and do anything."

Common characteristics for all terriers are their desire to work with great enthusiasm and courage. They all have large and powerful teeth for the size of their bodies, keen hearing, and excellent eyesight. No matter how many generations they have been pets, the purpose for which the breed was bred will remain with the dog.

The temperament of the Scottish Terrier is all terrier. He is quick, alert, intelligent, and robust. The Scot, however, is a bit less rambunctious than other terrier breeds, and has a tendency to be a one-family dog. He likes attention but doesn't want to be overwhelmed. He will sit or lie next to you,

Less rambunctious than other terriers, the Scottie has a dignified temperament and is known as a one-family dog. *Photo: Isabelle Francais*

The Scottish Terrier has a determined nature and a no-nonsense attitude. Despite his size, he will quickly defend his territory and family. *Photo: Isabelle Francais*

but he may not want to sit on your lap. He enjoys a good game or a giggle with his master, but he doesn't like to be made fun of.

Always laugh with him and not at him. He is sensitive to praise and to blame. He can adjust easily to children, but children must understand his independent nature and his sense of dignity. Unlike a Golden Retriever, this is not a pet to be hauled around, to have his ears pulled, or to be ridden upon. He enjoys walks with his family, retrieving a toss of the tennis ball, and quiet nights by the fire. He will ask little of you but a bit of love and some conversation. The Scottish Terrier has a tendency to be a bit stubborn. Scotties are independent, with minds of their own, and they obey grudgingly and at their own speed.

They can quickly figure out what is expected of them and just as quickly work their way around your expectations. They have proven to be a challenge for those who work with them in obedience, thus you will not see as many Scottie obedience champions as in some other terrier breeds. Scottie owners who work their dogs in obedience often feel that although their dog may not have achieved the title of companion dog, they themselves have learned a great deal of humility.

Scotties are basically no-nonsense dogs. They will not stand in the yard and bark for hours as some breeds will, and they will usually bark only when they hear a noise and want to alert their owners. The Scottie is a natural-born fighter. He will stand his ground but his actions will usually be defensive, protecting his territory as a sentinel.

S. S. Van Dyne, a famous mystery writer and breeder of Scottish Terriers, wrote: "A gentleman! This is perhaps the whole story. The Scottie is a gentleman. He is reserved, honorable, patient, tolerant, and courageous. He doesn't annoy you or force himself upon you. He meets life as he finds it, with an instinctive philosophy, a stoical intrepidity and a mellow understanding. He is calm and firm, and he minds his own business and minds it well. He is a Spartan and can suffer pain without whimpering, which is more than the majority of human beings can do. He will attack a lion or a tiger if his rights are invaded, and though he may die in the struggle he never shows the white feather or runs away. He is the most admirable of all sports, forthright, brave,

Stubborn and independent, the Scottie can prove to be a challenge to train. However, because of his intelligence, he can learn what you wish to teach him. *Photo: Isabelle Francais*

and uncomplaining. You know exactly where you stand with a Scottie."

COAT COLORS OF THE SCOTTISH TERRIER

Scottish Terriers come in three basic coat colors: black, brindle, and wheaten. The general public often assumes that all Scots are black, and when picking out a puppy they will insist, "I will only have a black Scottie."

The AKC registration application lists the following six colors: Black; Silver brindle; Brindle; Black brindle; Wheaten; and Red brindle. The definition of brindle is applied loosely to all coats that are not one self-color throughout. When two colors are listed, the first color is the dominant color. Thus, a black and (with) brindle Scot will

A true terrier at heart, the Scottie retains the tough exterior, instincts, and hunting abilities for which he was originally bred.
Photo: Isabelle Francais

often look like a black Scot to a novice, as the primary color is black. A gray and brindle will often be called a silver brindle. The wheaten should be the color of golden wheat or ripe corn. All colors are acceptable except white.

Puppy owners should be aware of the color range and know that there is no difference in the Scot underneath the coat, even if the outer coats are of a different color. The original Scots were primarily of the brindle shadings and occasionally, in the early days, there would be a white patch on the chest. On rare occasions, one will still see a small white blaze on the chest. Puppies with tufts of white on their chin or chest will lose these markings as they mature.

If you are purchasing your first Scottie, keep an open mind when it comes to color. Black and all the shades of brindle and

The Scottish Terrier's coat comes in three basic colors: black, brindle, and wheaten. These two Scotties show off their black and wheaten colors. *Photo: Isabelle Francais*

wheaten are equally desirable. The most important factor in your purchase is that you are buying a well-bred, healthy pup that has a disposition you like. Breeding, disposition, and health are factors that should be considered before coat color preference.

Although black is the most popular color, keep in mind that a puppy of any color variation, except white, is equally desirable and acceptable. *Photo: Isabelle Francais*

The Standard for the Scottish Terrier

General Appearance—The Scottish Terrier is a small, compact, short-legged, sturdily-built dog of good bone and substance. His head is long in proportion to his size. He has a hard, wiry, weather-resistant coat and a thick-set, cobby body which is hung between short, heavy legs. These characteristics, joined with his very special keen, piercing, "varminty" expression, and his erect ears and tail are salient features of the breed. The Scottish Terrier's bold, confident, dignified aspect exemplifies power in a small package.

Size, Proportion, Substance—The Scottish Terrier should have a thick body and heavy bone. The principal objective must be symmetry and balance without exaggeration. Equal consideration shall be given to height, weight, length of back and length of head. Height at withers for either sex should be about 10 inches. The length of back from withers to set-on of tail should be approximately 11 inches. Generally, a well-balanced Scottish Terrier dog should weigh from 19 to 22 pounds and a bitch from 18 to 21 pounds.

Head—The head should be long in proportion to the overall length and size of the dog. In profile, the skull and muzzle should give the appearance of two parallel planes. The *skull* should be long and of medium width, slightly domed and covered with short, hard hair. In profile, the skull should appear flat. There should be a slight but definite stop between the skull and

The Scottish Terrier is a small, compact, sturdy dog that exudes power and stamina.
Photo: Isabelle Francais

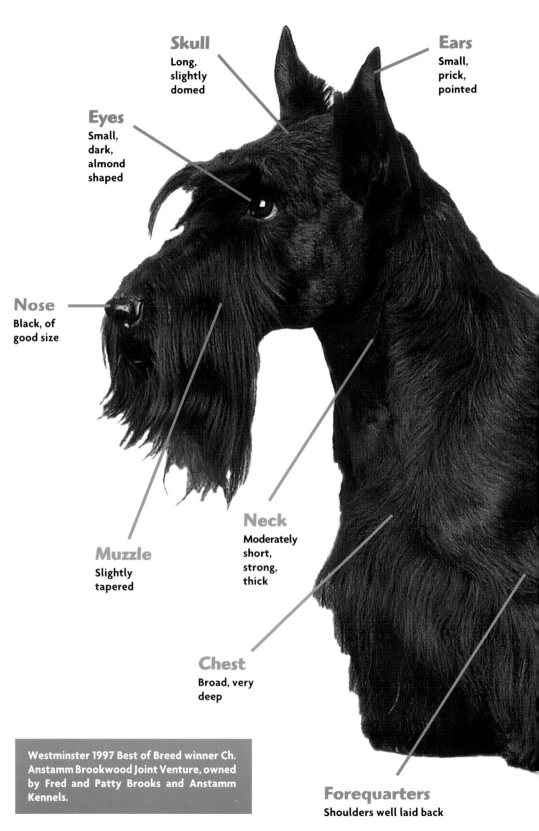

Skull
Long, slightly domed

Ears
Small, prick, pointed

Eyes
Small, dark, almond shaped

Nose
Black, of good size

Neck
Moderately short, strong, thick

Muzzle
Slightly tapered

Chest
Broad, very deep

Westminster 1997 Best of Breed winner Ch. Anstamm Brookwood Joint Venture, owned by Fred and Patty Brooks and Anstamm Kennels.

Forequarters
Shoulders well laid back

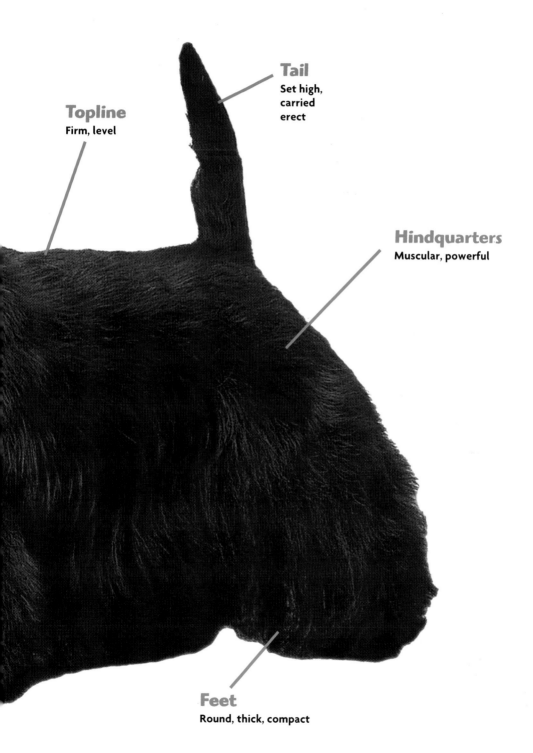

Topline
Firm, level

Tail
Set high,
carried
erect

Hindquarters
Muscular, powerful

Feet
Round, thick, compact

muzzle at eye level, allowing the eyes to be set in under the brow, contributing to proper Scottish Terrier expression. The skull should be smooth with no prominences or depressions and the cheeks should be flat and clean. The *muzzle* should be approximately equal to the length of skull with only a slight taper to the nose. The muzzle should be well filled in under the eye, with no evidence of snippiness. A correct Scottish Terrier muzzle should fill an average man's hand. The *nose* should be black, regardless of coat color, and of good size, projecting somewhat over the mouth and giving the impression that the upper jaw is longer than the lower. The *teeth* should be large and evenly spaced, having either a scissor or level bite, the former

The Scottie's head is long in proportion to his overall length and size and has a keen and intelligent expression. *Photo: Isabelle Francais*

preferred. The jaw should be square, level and powerful. Undershot or overshot bites should be penalized. The *eyes* should be set wide apart and well in under the brow. They should be small, bright and piercing, and almond-shaped not round. The color should be dark brown or nearly black, the darker the better. The *ears* should be small, prick, set well up on the skull and pointed, but never cut. They should be covered with short velvety hair. From the front, the outer edge of the ear should form a straight line up from the side of the skull. The use, size, shape and placement of the ear and its erect carriage are major elements of the keen, alert, intelligent Scottish Terrier expression.

Neck, Topline, Body—The neck should be moderately short, strong, thick and muscular, blending smoothly into well laid back shoulders. The neck must never be so short as to appear clumsy. The *body* should be moderately short with ribs extending well back into a short, strong loin, deep flanks and very muscular hindquarters. The ribs should be well sprung out from the spine, forming a broad, strong back, then curving down and inward to form a deep body that would be nearly heart-shaped if viewed in cross-section. The *topline* of the back should be firm and level. The *chest* should be broad, very deep and well let down between the forelegs. The forechest should extend well in front of the legs and drop well down into the brisket. The chest should not be flat or concave, and the brisket should nicely fill an average man's slightly cupped hand. The lowest point of

The topline of the Scottish Terrier should be firm and level, and his chest broad and very deep.
Photo: Isabelle Francais

the brisket should be such that an average man's fist would fit under it with little or no overhead clearance. The *tail* should be about seven inches long and never cut. It should be set on high and carried erectly, either vertical or with a slight curve forward, but not over the back. The tail should be thick at the base, tapering gradually to a point and covered with short, hard hair.

Forequarters—The shoulders should be well laid back and moderately well knit at the withers. The forelegs should be very heavy in bone, straight or slightly bent with elbows close to the body, and set in under the shoulder blade with a definite forechest in front of them. Scottish Terriers should not be out at the elbows. The forefeet should be larger than the hind feet, round,

thick and compact with strong nails. The front feet should point straight ahead, but a slight "toeing out" is acceptable. Dew claws may be removed.

Hindquarters—The thighs should be very muscular and powerful for the size of the dog with the stifles well bent and the legs straight from hock to heel. Hocks should be well let down and parallel to each other.

Coat—The Scottish Terrier should have a broken coat. It is a hard, wiry outer coat with a soft, dense undercoat. The coat should be trimmed and blended into the furnishings to give a distinct Scottish Terrier outline. The dog should be presented with sufficient coat so that the texture and density may be determined. The longer coat on the beard, legs and lower body may be slightly softer than the body coat but should not be or appear fluffy.

Color—Black, wheaten or brindle of any color. Many black and brindle dogs have sprinklings of white or silver hairs in their coats which are normal and not to be penalized. White can be allowed only on the chest and chin and that to a slight extent only.

Gait—The gait of the Scottish Terrier is very characteristic of the breed. It is not the square trot or walk desirable in the long-legged breeds. The forelegs do not move in exact parallel planes; rather, in reaching out, the forelegs incline slightly inward because of the deep broad forechest. Movement should be free, agile and coordinated with powerful drive from the rear and good reach in front. The action of the rear legs should be square and true and, at the trot, both the hocks and stifles should be flexed with a vigorous motion. When the dog is in motion, the back should remain firm and level.

Temperament—The Scottish Terrier should be alert and spirited but also stable and steady-going. He is a determined and thoughtful dog whose "heads up, tails up" attitude in the ring should convey both fire and control. The Scottish Terrier, while loving and gentle with people, can be aggressive with other dogs. He should exude ruggedness and power, living up to his nickname, the "Diehard."

Penalties—Soft coat; curly coat; round, protruding or light eyes; overshot or undershot jaws; obviously oversize or undersize; shyness or timidity; upright shoulders; lack of reach in front or drive in rear; stiff or stilted movement; movement too wide or too close in rear; too narrow in front or rear; out at the elbow; lack of bone and substance; low set tail; lack of pigment in

The naturally short tail of the Scottish Terrier should be set high and carried erect.
Photo: Isabelle Francais

THE GUIDE TO OWNING A SCOTTISH TERRIER

The Scottish Terrier has a double coat consisting of a hard, wiry outercoat and a soft, dense undercoat that should be blended into the furnishing to create a distinct outline. *Photo: Isabelle Francais*

the nose; coarse head; and failure to show with head and tail up are faults to be penalized.

NO JUDGE SHOULD PUT TO WINNERS OR BEST OF BREED ANY SCOTTISH TERRIER NOT SHOWING REAL TERRIER CHARACTER IN THE RING.

Scale of Points

Skull 5

Muzzle 5

Eyes 5

Ears 10

Neck 5

Chest 5

Body 15

Legs & Feet 10

Tail 5

Coat 15

Size 10

General Appearance 10

Approved October 12, 1993

Effective November 30, 1993

Although black is the most popular, wheaten and brindle are also accepted coat colors of the Scottish Terrier. *Photo: Isabelle Francais*

Alert and spirited, the Scottie should possess a stable temperament and a rugged demeanor.
Photo: Isabelle Francais

THE GUIDE TO OWNING A SCOTTISH TERRIER

Feeding Your Scottish Terrier

Now let's talk about feeding your Scottish Terrier, a subject so simple that it's amazing there is so much nonsense and misunderstanding about it. Is it expensive to feed a Scottish Terrier? No, it is not! You can feed your Scottie economically and keep him in perfect shape the year round, or you can feed him expensively. He'll thrive either way, and let's see why this is true.

First, remember that a Scottish Terrier is a dog. Dogs do not have a high degree of selectivity in their food, and unless you spoil them with great variety (and possibly turn them into poor, "picky" eaters) they

The Scottie is a hardy dog that will thrive with the proper diet and care. *Photo: Isabelle Francais*

will eat almost anything that they become accustomed to. Many dogs flatly refuse to eat nice, fresh beef. They pick around it and eat everything else. But meat—bah! Why? They aren't accustomed to it. They'd eat rabbit fast enough, but they refuse beef because they aren't used to it.

VARIETY IS NOT NECESSARY

A good general rule of thumb is forget all human preferences and don't give a thought to variety. Choose the right diet for your Scottie and feed it to him day after day, year after year, winter and summer. But what is the right diet?

Hundreds of thousands of dollars have been spent in canine nutrition research. The results are pretty conclusive, so you needn't go into a lot of experimenting with trials of this and that every other week.

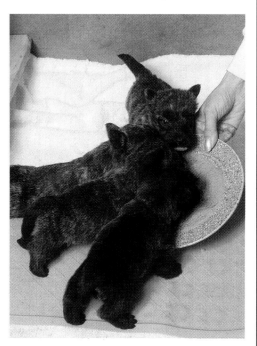

Choose a dog food that is especially formulated for your Scottie's stage of life. Puppies will need a growth formula. *Photo: Isabelle Francais*

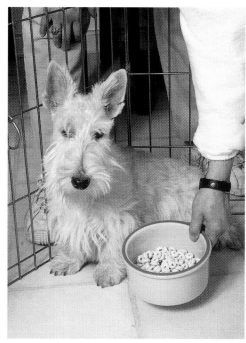

Once you have chosen a nutritious, good-quality dog food, stick with it and make any changes in your Scottie's diet very gradually. *Photo: Isabelle Francais*

Research has proven just what your dog needs to eat and to keep healthy.

DOG FOOD

There are almost as many right diets as there are dog experts, but the basic diet most often recommended is one that consists of a dry food, either meal or kibble form. There are several of excellent quality, manufactured by reliable companies, research tested, and nationally advertised. They are inexpensive, highly satisfactory, and easily available in stores everywhere in containers of 5 to 50 pounds. Larger amounts usually cost less per pound.

If you have a choice of brands, it is generally safer to choose the better-known one; but even so, carefully read the analysis on the package. Do not choose any food in which the protein level is less than 25 percent, and be sure that this protein comes from both animal and vegetable sources. The good dog foods have meat meal, fish meal, liver, and such, plus protein from alfalfa and soy beans, as well as some dried-milk product. Note the vitamin content carefully. See that they are all there in good proportions; and be especially certain that the food contains properly high levels of vitamins A and D, two of the most perishable and important ones. Note the B-complex level, but don't worry about carbohydrate and mineral levels. These substances are plentiful and cheap and not likely to be lacking in a good brand.

The advice given for how to choose a dry food also applies to moist or canned types of dog foods, if you decide to feed one of these.

Having chosen a really good food, feed it to your Scottish Terrier as the manufacturer directs. And once you've started, stick to it. Never change if you can possibly help it. A switch from one meal or kibble-type food can usually be made without too much upset; however, a change will almost invariably give you (and your Scottie) some trouble.

WHEN SUPPLEMENTS ARE NEEDED

Now what about supplements of various kinds, mineral and vitamin, or the various oils? They are all okay to add to your Scottie's food. However, if you are feeding your dog a correct diet, and this is easy to do, no supplements are necessary unless your Scottish Terrier has been improperly fed, has been sick, or is having puppies. Vitamins and minerals are naturally present

If you choose to give your Scottie treats, make sure they are nutritious and do not upset his regular diet.
Photo: Isabelle Francais

If you put your Scottish Terrier on a regular feeding schedule, he will always know when it is mealtime.
Photo: Isabelle Francais

in all the foods; and to ensure against any loss through processing, they are added in concentrated form to the dog food you use. Except on the advice of your veterinarian, added amounts of vitamins can prove harmful to your Scottie. The same risk goes with minerals.

FEEDING SCHEDULE
When and how much food to give your Scottish Terrier? Most dogs do better if fed two or three smaller meals per day—this is not only better but vital to larger and deep-chested dogs. As to how to prepare the food and how much to give, it is generally best to follow the directions on the food package. Your own Scottish Terrier may want a little more or a little less.

Fresh, cool water should always be available to your Scottish Terrier. This is important to good health throughout his lifetime.

ALL SCOTTISH TERRIERS NEED TO CHEW
Puppies and young Scottish Terriers need something with resistance to chew on while their teeth and jaws are developing—for cutting the puppy teeth, to induce growth of the permanent teeth under the puppy teeth, to assist in getting rid of the puppy teeth at the proper time, to help the permanent teeth through the gums, to ensure normal jaw development, and to settle the permanent teeth solidly in the jaws.

The adult Scottish Terrier's desire to chew stems from the instinct for tooth cleaning, gum massage, and jaw exercise—plus the need for an outlet for periodic doggie tensions.

This is why dogs, especially puppies and young dogs, will often destroy property worth hundreds of dollars when their chewing instinct is not diverted from their owner's possessions. And this is why you should provide your Scottish Terrier with something to chew—something that has the necessary functional qualities, is desirable from the Scottish Terrier's viewpoint, and is safe for him.

It is very important that your Scottish Terrier not be permitted to chew on anything he can break or on any indigestible thing from which he can bite sizable chunks. Sharp pieces, such as from a bone that can be broken by a dog, may pierce the intestinal wall and kill. Indigestible things that can be bitten off in chunks, such as from shoes or rubber or plastic toys, may cause an intestinal stoppage (if not regurgitated) and bring painful death, unless surgery is promptly performed.

Strong natural bones, such as 4- to 8-inch lengths of round shin bone from mature beef—either the kind you can get from a butcher or one of the variety available commercially in pet stores—may serve your Scottish Terrier's teething needs if his mouth is large enough to handle them effectively. You may be tempted to give your Scottish Terrier puppy a smaller bone and he may not be able to break it when you do, but puppies grow rapidly and the power of their jaws constantly increases until maturity. This means that a growing Scottish Terrier may break one of the smaller bones at any time, swallow the pieces, and die painfully before you realize what is wrong.

All hard natural bones are very abrasive. If your Scottish Terrier is an avid chewer, natural bones may wear away his teeth prematurely; hence, they then should be taken away from your dog when the teething purposes have been served. The badly worn, and usually painful, teeth of many mature dogs can be traced to excessive chewing on natural bones.

Providing your Scottie with safe chew toys will help keep his teeth and jaws occupied.
Photo: Isabelle Francais

It is wise to train your Scottie to have good chewing habits while he is a puppy, then he will have healthy teeth throughout his life. *Photo: Isabelle Francais*

Contrary to popular belief, knuckle bones that can be chewed up and swallowed by your Scottish Terrier provide little, if any, usable calcium or other nutriment. They do, however, disturb the digestion of most dogs and cause them to vomit the nourishing food they need.

Dried rawhide products of various types, shapes, sizes, and prices are available on the market and have become quite popular. However, they don't serve the primary chewing functions very well; they are a bit messy when wet from mouthing, and most Scottish Terriers chew them up rather rapidly—but they have been considered safe for dogs until recently. Now, more and more incidents of death, and near death, by asphyxiation have been reported to be the results of partially swallowed chunks of rawhide swelling in the throat. More recently, some veterinarians have been attributing cases of acute constipation to large pieces of incompletely digested rawhide in the intestine.

A new product, molded rawhide, is very safe. During the process, the rawhide is melted and then injection molded into the familiar dog shape. It is very hard and is eagerly accepted by Scottish Terriers. The melting process also sterilizes the rawhide. Don't confuse this with pressed rawhide, which is nothing more than small strips of rawhide squeezed together.

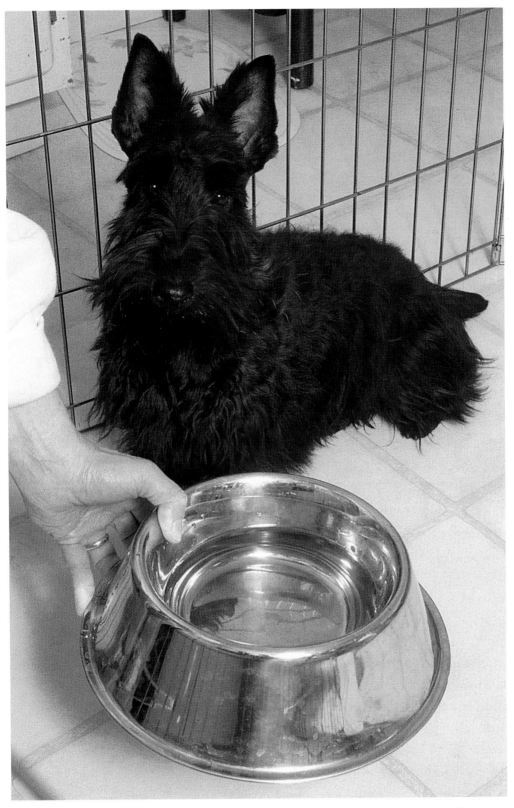

Your Scottish Terrier should have cool, clean water accessible to him at all times. *Photo: Isabelle Francais*

The toughness of the nylon provides the strong chewing resistance needed for important jaw exercise and effectively aids teething functions, but there is no tooth wear because nylon is nonabrasive. Being inert, nylon does not support the growth of microorganisms, and it can be washed in soap and water or it can be sterilized by boiling or in an autoclave.

Nylabone® is highly recommended by veterinarians as a safe, healthy nylon bone that can't splinter or chip. Nylabone® is frizzled by the dog's chewing action, creating a toothbrush-like surface that cleanses the teeth and massages the gums.

Your Scottie's nutritious diet will be evident in his overall healthy appearance.
Photo: Isabelle Francais

The nylon bones, especially those with natural meat and bone fractions added, are probably the most complete, safe, and economical answer to the chewing need. Dogs cannot break them or bite off sizable chunks; and being longer lasting than other things offered for the purpose, they are affordable.

Hard chewing raises little bristle-like projections on the surface of the nylon bones in order to provide effective interim teeth cleaning and vigorous gum massage, much in the same way your toothbrush does for you. The little projections are raked off and swallowed in the form of thin shavings, but the chemistry of the nylon is such that they break down in the stomach fluids and pass through without effect.

Toys are an excellent way to relieve your Scottie's need to chew while keeping your dog and your belongings safe. *Photo: Isabelle Francais*

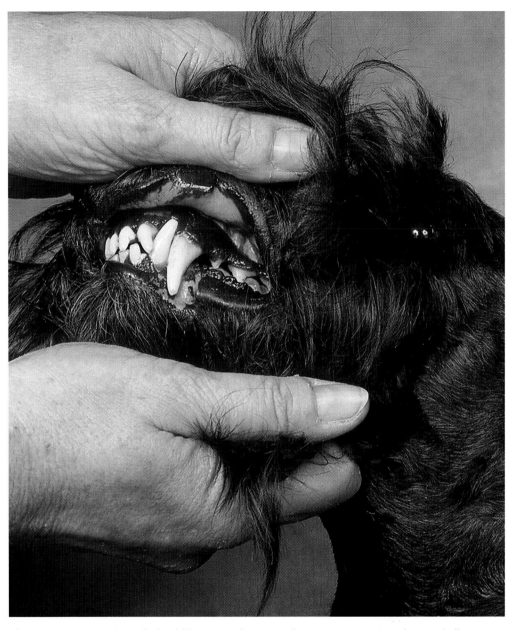

Cleaning your Scottie's teeth should be a part of your regular grooming routine. *Photo: Isabelle Francais*

Nylabone® is superior to the cheaper bones because it is made of virgin nylon, which is the strongest and longest-lasting type of nylon available. The cheaper bones are made from recycled or reground nylon scraps, and have a tendency to break apart and split easily.

Nothing, however, substitutes for periodic professional attention for your Scottie's teeth and gums, not any more than your toothbrush can do that for you. Have your Scottish Terrier's teeth cleaned at least once a year by your veterinarian (twice a year is better) and your dog will be happier, healthier, and far more pleasant to live with.

Grooming Your Scottish Terrier

You must understand before purchasing your Scottish Terrier that this is a breed with a coat that needs maintenance, whether you have a dog for the show ring or one that is a household pet. Think of it in terms of your child—you bathe your youngster, comb his hair, and put a clean set of clothes on him. The end product is

Due to his double coat, your Scottish Terrier will need regular grooming to keep him looking his best.
Photo: Isabelle Francais

A slicker brush will be useful to brush out your Scottie and remove any dead hair or debris from his coat.
Photo: Isabelle Francais

that you have a child that smells good, that looks nice, and that you enjoy having in your company. It is the same with your dog—keep the dog brushed, cleaned, and trimmed, and you will find it a pleasure to be in his company. However, it will require some effort to do this.

The Scottie is a double-coated dog. There is a dense, thick undercoat that protects the dog in all kinds of weather and a harsh outercoat. Coat care for the pet Scottie can be much different and easier than the coat care for a show dog. The vast majority of Scottie fanciers have a pet dog, and they should not expect to maintain a show coat.

If you are planning to show your Scottish Terrier, you will be ahead of the game if you purchase your puppy from a reputable breeder who grooms and shows her dogs. If so, this is the individual to see for grooming lessons to learn how to get your dog ready for the show ring. Grooming for the show is an art, and it is an art that cannot be learned in a few months. Furthermore, it is very difficult but not impossible to learn it from a book.

The primary difference between the pet and show Scottie coat is that the show Scottie will have a dense undercoat, and on top of it he will have a shiny, harsh coat that will fit him like a jacket. With the proper coat, the dog presents a smartness in the ring that can be hard to beat. This coat can only be acquired by

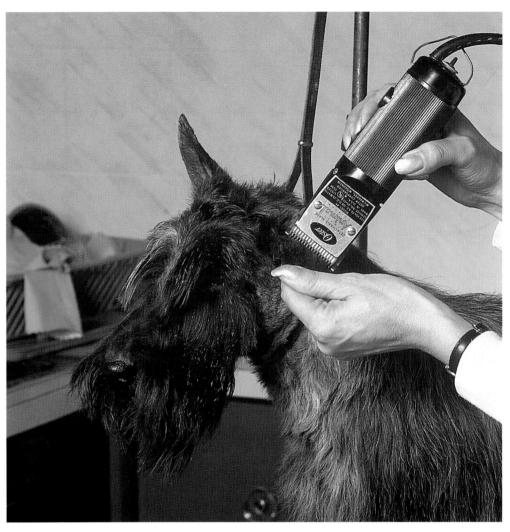

A Scottie's coat will need to be clipped approximately every three months, especially around the head and neck. *Photo: Isabelle Francais*

stripping the body coat with a stripping knife or stripping by hand. With the proper upkeep, he will have grown from his "underwear" outfit stage into a smart new outfit ready for the ring within 10 to 12 weeks. This all takes skill, time, and interest in order to do it well.

Pet grooming is different from grooming for the show ring, as you use a clipper on the body and scissors for trimming the furnishings. You will not have the harsh, tight-fitting jacket of the show Scot, but

you will have a neat, clean, and trimmed dog that will still look like a Scottish Terrier. Even those with kennels that have dogs that are active in the show ring will clip their old dogs or those who are no longer being shown.

Here are the tools that you will need if you are going to do your own grooming:

1. A grooming table, something sturdy with a rubber mat covering the top. You will need a grooming arm or a hangar. (You can use a table in your laundry room with an

eye hook in the ceiling for holding the leash.) Your dog will now be comfortable even if confined and you will be able to work on him. Grooming is a very difficult and frustrating job if you try to groom without a table and a grooming arm.

2. A metal comb, a slicker brush, a good, sharp pair of scissors, and a toenail trimmer.

3. Electric clippers with a #10 blade.

To start: Set your dog on the table and put the leash around his neck. Have your leash up behind the ears and pull it taut when you fasten it to your eye hook. Do not walk away and leave your dog unattended, because he could jump off the table and be left dangling from the leash with his feet scrambling around in the air.

Take your slicker brush and brush out the entire coat. Brush the whiskers toward the nose, the body hair toward the tail, and the tail up toward the tip of the tail. Brush the leg furnishings up toward the body, and brush the chest hair down toward the table. Hold the dog up by the front legs and gently brush the stomach hair, first toward the head and then back toward the rear. For cleanliness, you may want to take your scissors and trim the area around the penis. With the girls, trim some of the hair around the vulva. Now that your dog is brushed

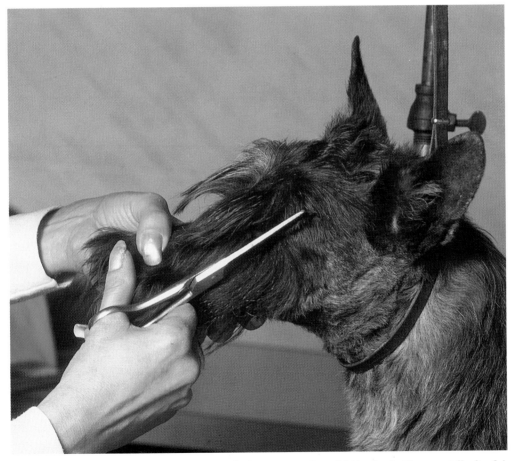

Scissors can be used to trim any excess hair or whiskers on your Scottish Terrier, but be especially careful around his face and eyes. *Photo: Isabelle Francais*

If you accustom your Scottish Terrier puppy to grooming procedures at a young age, he should come to accept them as routine.
Photo: Isabelle Francais

out, comb through the coat with your metal comb.

By now you have removed a fair amount of dead hair and your dog will already look better. You may find some small mats and these can be worked out with your fingers or your comb. If you brush your dog out every week or so, you will not have too much of a problem with the mats.

We are now at the stage where you will take your clippers in hand. Your dog will only need to be clipped every three months or so, but you may want to touch up the head more often. Start with the head and follow this pattern: Take your clippers and clip the neck, shoulders, and body, following the grooming illustrations. Be sure to trim in the direction that the hair lays. Now, take your comb and comb the leg hair down toward the table. Take your scissors and trim the legs neatly.

Next, take your scissors and trim off anything that "sticks out." If this is your first experience, you may be a bit clumsy, but the hair will grow back in a short time. The finished product may not be quite what you had expected, but expertise will come with experience and you will soon be very proud of your efforts. Your dog should now look like a Scottish Terrier.

Put your dog in the laundry tub when you are finished and give him a good bath and rinsing. After toweling him down, return him to the grooming table and trim the toenails on all four feet. At this point, you can dry your dog with a hair dryer and brush him out again, or you can let him dry naturally and then brush him out.

If you have grooming problems, you can take your dog to the professional groomer the first time or two for his grooming. The groomer will "set" the pattern, and then it will be easier for you to get the Scottie look by following the pattern that is already set in the coat. (Of course, you can eliminate all of the grooming for yourself, except for the weekly brushing, if you take your dog to the groomer every three months!) If the coat totally grows out before you start to groom, the pattern will be lost and then you will have to start over again. Just remember that many pet owners can do a much better job trimming their dogs than some professional groomers.

To wrap it up: Your pet should be brushed weekly and bathed as needed. Trim the toenails every month or so and plan to clip the dog every three months. Follow this plan and your dog will not only be clean, he also will have a new dress every three months, and he will look like a Scottish Terrier!

You should always inspect your Scottie's feet when grooming and keep his toenails short to avoid injuries. *Photo: Isabelle Francais*

Training Your Scottish Terrier

You owe proper training to your Scottish Terrier. The right and privilege of being trained are his birthright. Whether your Scottish Terrier is going to be a handsome, well-mannered housedog and companion, a show dog, or whatever possible use he may be put to, the basic training is always the same—all must start with basic obedience, or what might be called "manner training."

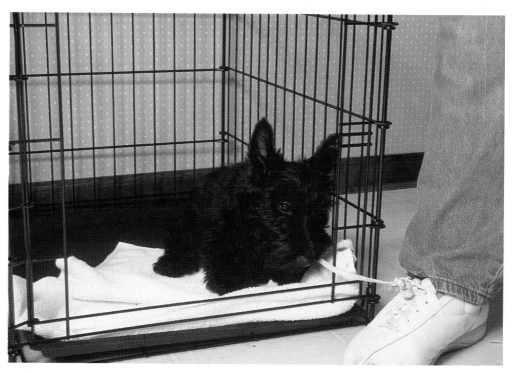

Little puppies can get in a lot of trouble. Establishing discipline in the beginning of your relationship will help your puppy to know that you are the leader. *Photo: Isabelle Francais*

Your Scottish Terrier needs your guidance and discipline in order to help him learn the household rules.
Photo: Isabelle Francais

Training classes are a great place to teach your Scottie basic obedience, as well as socialize him with other dogs. *Photo: Isabelle Francais*

Your Scottish Terrier must come instantly when called and obey the "Sit" or "Down" command just as fast; he must walk quietly at "Heel," whether on or off lead. He must be mannerly and polite wherever he goes; he must be polite to strangers on the street and in stores. He must be mannerly in the presence of other dogs. He must not bark at children on roller skates, motorcycles, or other domestic animals. And he must be restrained from chasing cats. It is not a dog's inalienable right to chase cats, and he must be reprimanded for it.

PROFESSIONAL TRAINING

How do you go about this training? Well, it's a very simple procedure, pretty well standardized by now. First, if you can afford the extra expense, you may send your Scottish Terrier to a professional trainer, where in 30 to 60 days he will learn how to be a "good dog." If you enlist the services of a good professional trainer, follow his advice of when to come to see the dog. No, he won't forget you, but too-frequent visits at the wrong time may slow down his training progress. And using a "pro" trainer means that you will have to go for some training, too, after the trainer feels your Scottish Terrier is ready to go home. You will have to learn how your Scottish Terrier works, just what to expect of him, and how to use what the dog has learned after he is home.

OBEDIENCE TRAINING CLASS

Another way to train your Scottish Terrier (many experienced Scottish Terrier people think this is the best) is to join an obedience training class right in your own community.

THE GUIDE TO OWNING A SCOTTISH TERRIER

There is such a group in nearly every community nowadays. Here you will be working with a group of people who are also just starting out. You will actually be training your own dog, since all work is done under the direction of a head trainer who will make suggestions to you and also tell you when and how to correct your Scottish Terrier's errors. Then, too, working with such a group, your Scottish Terrier will learn to get along with other dogs. And, what is more important, he will learn to do exactly what he is told to do, no matter how much confusion there is around him or how great the temptation is to go his own way.

Write to your national kennel club for the location of a training club or class in your locality. Sign up. Go to it regularly—every session! Go early and leave late! Both you and your Scottish Terrier will benefit tremendously.

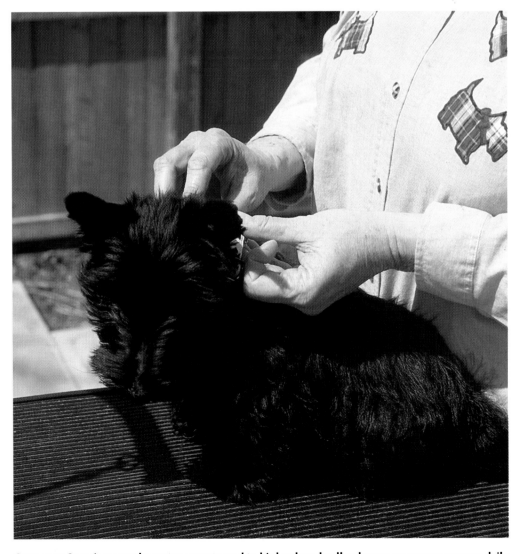

Once your Scottie puppy becomes accustomed to his leash and collar, he can accompany you on daily walks. *Photo: Isabelle Francais*

A tasty treat can be great motivation for your Scottie puppy when learning new commands. *Photo: Isabelle Francais*

TRAIN HIM BY THE BOOK

The third way of training your Scottish Terrier is by the book. Yes, you can do it this way and do a good job of it, too. But in using the book method, select a book, buy it, study it carefully; then study it some more, until the procedures are almost second nature to you. Then start your training. But stay with the book and its advice and exercises. Don't start in and then make up a few rules of your own. If you don't follow the book, you'll get into jams you can't get out of by yourself. If after a few hours of short training sessions your Scottish Terrier is still not working as he should, get back to the book for a study session, because it's your fault, not the dog's! The procedures of dog training have been so well systemized that it must be your fault, because literally thousands of fine Scottish Terriers have been trained by the book.

After your Scottish Terrier is "letter perfect" under all conditions, then, if you wish, go on to advanced training and trick work.

Your Scottish Terrier will love his obedience training, and you'll burst with pride at the finished product! He will enjoy life even more, and you'll enjoy his company greatly. And remember—you owe good training to your Scottish Terrier.

Crate training is the fastest and easiest way to housebreak your Scottish Terrier. *Photo: Isabelle Francais*

Showing Your Scottish Terrier

Dog shows have been in existence in America for well over 100 years. The Westminster Kennel Club dog show, held every year in the beginning of February in New York City, is the second oldest annual sporting event in the country, with only the Kentucky Derby having greater longevity.

If you are new to the show ring, attend a few local shows without your dog to see what the game is about. If you are competitive, have the time and the money to compete, and of course, have a good dog, this may be the sport and hobby for you.

If you have not already done so, join your local Scottish Terrier club. This is really a must for a novice in the ring. The local club will hold one or two seminars a year on grooming for the show ring, in addition to having match shows where you can learn how to show your dog. Match shows are run like a dog show, but they are casual and a good place for the beginner to learn. You will not receive any points toward a championship, but you will find out how a dog show is run and learn what will be expected of you and your dog. Entry fees are minimal. This is also a good opportunity to meet the people in the breed.

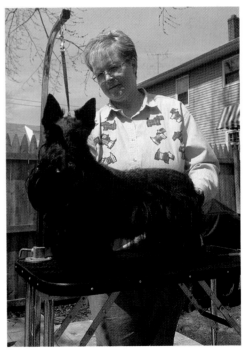

Your Scottish Terrier will have to become used to extensive grooming if he is to compete in conformation shows. *Photo: Isabelle Francais*

Once your Scottie has mastered basic obedience, he can go on to compete in more advanced training. *Photo: Isabelle Francais*

Contact your local all-breed club and find out if they offer conformation classes where you can learn how to handle your dog in the ring. Start attending these classes on a regular basis. One class does not an expert make! Your all-breed club will hold one or two matches a year and you should plan to attend these matches.

When you think you are ready—your dog is in coat and can walk on a lead, and you feel a tiny bit of confidence—enter an AKC-licensed dog show.

Remember that participating successfully in dog shows requires patience, time, money, skill, and talent. It is the only sport where the amateur and the professional compete on an equal footing. The average dog show competitor remains active for only four to five years. Personal commitments such as children, work, and other hobbies can be a problem for those who want to compete every weekend. More often, the competitor who does not win enough will find his interest in the sport waning. A poorly groomed dog, a poorly bred dog, a dog that does not like to show, and a handler who will not take the time to learn how to handle well are all deterrents to staying with the sport of dog showing.

WORKING WITH A SCOTTISH TERRIER

Every Scottish Terrier should be able to lie around the house, have a good meal, receive love and attention, and be taken for a walk or a romp every day. However, some owners like the challenge of working with their

Training your Scottie for dog sports can give both you and your dog a great sense of accomplishment and can help build a stronger bond between you. *Photo: Isabelle Francais*

dog, training him to follow commands, and seeing him perform the chores that he was bred to do. With terriers, an owner can work in obedience, train in agility, or send his dog to ground in a working trial. It is surely challenging to work a Scot but it can be done, and an owner can have a tremendous feeling of accomplishment once a goal is set and reached.

OBEDIENCE

Scotties are not an easy breed to work with in obedience. With their intelligence and independent spirit, they can sometimes be more trying to train than had been anticipated. You will see Golden Retrievers, Poodles, and Miniature Schnauzers in abundance in obedience classes, because these are breeds that are easy to work with. Not only are they intelligent, but more importantly, they have a willingness to please their master. Scotties don't always want to please, and they can quickly become bored with working the same exercise over and over again.

In spite of these difficulties, Scotties do complete obedience degrees and some individuals have been very successful with training them up to the highest degree of work, the Utility degree.

For obedience work, dog and handler need aptitude and determination. The handler must take time to work his dog every day, even if it is only for five minutes or so. The handler must also have patience, and the dog must have a desire to perform

Because of their high degree of intelligence and independent nature, Scotties can be a challenge to train in obedience. However, with patience and the right motivation, they can excel in advanced competition.
Photo: Isabelle Francais

Successful showing requires dedication and preparation, but most of all, it should be enjoyable for both dog and handler. *Photo: Isabelle Francais*

and at least some willingness to please. Once this match is made, a handler and his dog can be well on their way toward an obedience degree, and the handler will feel a tremendous amount of achievement and accomplishment to have such a smart little dog working by his side.

Spectators at a dog show love to watch the obedience rings, because they can understand what the dog is doing (or not doing) much better than when they watch the conformation rings. There is no better sight than watching the Scot, with his short legs, flying over the hurdles.

Obedience classes are offered throughout the country, and unless you live in a very remote area, your town or city should offer you a selection of training clubs. Some classes are offered by private individuals, others by obedience clubs or all-breed clubs. There are different methods of instruction and you may find it

worthwhile to visit various classes to see which method of training you prefer.

AGILITY

Agility is a relatively new sport that has come to the United States from England. The handler and the dog, working as a team, go through a timed obstacle course. Scoring is simple and objective, based upon the dog's completing all of the obstacles at the speed with which this is accomplished.

In order to compete in this sport, you must belong to an all-breed club or an obedience club where there are individuals who support this event. The obstacle course requires substantial space and the obstacles themselves are fairly extensive.

Many dog shows now hold agility as an exhibition. The ring is easy to find as spectators can be four deep around the entire area. A great deal of enthusiasm

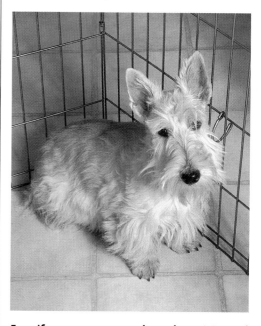

Even if you never enter a show, the training and attention you give your Scottie can only benefit him in the long run. *Photo: Isabelle Francais*

Originally, the Scottie was bred to be a working terrier. Those instincts still remain with him to this day and allow him to excel in working trials. *Photo: Isabelle Francais*

emanates from all quarters: cheers from the spectators, barking from the dogs, and loud encouragement from the handlers. This is a fun sport and not for the weak of heart!

WORKING TRIALS

Scottish Terriers are bred to go to ground after vermin and small rodents. Even if most dogs have not been required to use these skills on an everyday basis, the instinct remains in a well-bred Scot. Everyone is familiar with the rapt attention that a Scottie will give a squirrel that crosses his path, the quick way the Scot will find a mouse in the kennel, or the speed with which he can flush out a rabbit in a field. The short-legged terriers were used to drag the prey out of their dens or to force the vermin to bolt from their dens. On occasion, they would hold the prey at bay to indicate the location for their master.

Working trials, like obedience trials, are open to dogs of all ages. Again, the sport requires a willingness to compete on the Scot's part and the usual patience and perseverance on the owner's part.

THERAPY DOG

If you like to volunteer, it is wonderful if you can take your Scot to a nursing home once a week for several hours. The elder community loves to have a dog to visit with and often your dog will bring a bit of companionship to someone who is either lonely or who may be somewhat detached from the world. You will not only be bringing happiness to someone else, but you will be keeping your little dog busy—and we haven't even mentioned the fact that they have discovered that volunteering helps to increase your longevity!

A well-trained Scottish Terrier that has a good temperament can be a joy to have around and will be welcomed everywhere he goes. *Photo: Isabelle Francais*

THE GUIDE TO OWNING A SCOTTISH TERRIER

Your Healthy Scottish Terrier

By and large, the Scottish Terrier is considered to be a healthy breed, relatively free from genetic problems and often known for longevity.

William Haynes wrote in 1925, "The terrier owner is a 'lucky Devil' for his dogs do not, as a rule, spend a great deal of time in the hospital. All members of the terrier family, from the giant of the race, the Airedale, way down to little Scottie, owe a big debt to Nature for having blessed them with remarkably robust constitutions. Even when really sick, they make wonderfully rapid recoveries. It is almost a joke to keep such a naturally healthy dog as a terrier in the pink of condition. All he needs are dry, clean kennels with decent bedding; a good, nourishing food at regular hours; all the fresh water he wants to drink; plenty of exercise; and a little grooming. Given these few things and a terrier will be disgustingly well, full of high spirits, and happy as a clam at high tide."

A Scottie is a thrifty dog. Give him care, use your common sense, and have a good veterinarian available. Find a reliable veterinarian that you trust, take your dog in

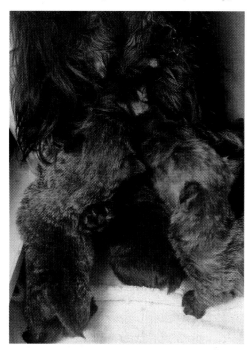

Puppies will get their first immunities from nursing. After they are weaned, however, they will need immunizations to protect them from disease. *Photo: Isabelle Francais*

when you think that he has a problem, follow instructions, and recovery will usually be very rapid.

Your dog should have yearly inoculations along with having a stool sample run to make certain that he is free from worms. Keep his teeth clean and his nails trimmed. Your veterinarian can do these jobs if you or your groomer are unable to do so. Watch for ticks in the summer and clean out any wounds immediately. Some of them may require veterinary care. Yearly heartworm checks in some areas of the country are also important.

If your veterinarian is not available at odd hours for emergencies, know where the emergency veterinarian is located and keep his telephone number handy. Many veterinarians in large cities no longer have an emergency service, and you must rely on these special facilities for late evening, weekend, and holiday services.

Keep your dog groomed and clean. Keep him out of the sun in the summer and certainly don't leave him in the car during a hot day. The Scottie's dark coat can soak up sun and heat and the two combined can cause severe heat problems for any dog.

Watch your Scot around the water. They are not good swimmers, probably due to their short legs. Many have drowned in swimming pools, unable to stay afloat or to climb out.

Your dog should be kept in either a fenced yard or on a leash. It's foolish and often against the law to let your dog run loose and take a chance of being run over by a car. Too often the story is heard about the dog that lives at the end of the cul-de-sac where

For their safety, keep your Scotties in a safe enclosure when you cannot supervise them.
Photo: Isabelle Francais

THE GUIDE TO OWNING A SCOTTISH TERRIER

Regular grooming is an excellent way to keep on top of any health problems or conditions that your Scottie may be experiencing. *Photo: Isabelle Francais*

only one delivery truck comes a day, and that truck runs over the dog. It only takes one vehicle to shorten a dog's life.

Dogs often live to seven or eight years and then die of some disease. It seems that if your Scot lives to eight years of age, your chances are good that you will have another two to six years with him. Eleven- and twelve-year-old Scotties are not unusual. Remember, anything after eight years, in any breed, is usually a gift.

A few particular Scottie problems should be mentioned. They are Scottie cramp, von Willebrand's disease, epileptic seizures, and cancer.

SCOTTIE CRAMP
Scottie cramp is an inherited neurological disorder that is seen only in the Scottish Terrier. Studies are still being done, but it appears to be carried by a recessive gene. It can show up in a pup as early as six to eight weeks of age, but more likely it will manifest at about six months. The Scottie will be running and playing hard and the rear legs will start to stiffen up (cramp). The body then becomes drawn up and arched, the forelegs stiffen, and the dog falls over. In a few seconds, he is back on his feet.

Dogs affected by Scottie cramp can be wonderful pets, and their condition can be reduced by giving affected dogs vitamin E or diazepam on a daily basis. Dogs exhibiting any degree of Scottie cramp should not be bred.

VON WILLEBRAND'S DISEASE
Von Willebrand's Disease (vWD) is the most common bleeding disorder of man and dogs and affects many breeds. This is an inherited disease carried by a recessive gene. Scotties can either be free of vWD, be carriers of the

gene, or be "bleeders." Reputable breeders have their animal's blood tested to make sure that they are not breeding dogs that have vWD or that carry the gene. Dogs that score 60 and above on their blood test are considered to test normal for the disease. Those that score in the 50 to 59 range are borderline normal and should be bred only to dogs with a normal score. Care should be taken in those that score below 50 and if the dog is bred, it should be bred to a dog that scores in the normal range for vWD.

SEIZURES

Epileptic seizures, convulsions, and "fits" are terms used to describe the same event—

A breeder's good care will be evident in the happy, healthy, well-adjusted puppies that are produced.
Photo: Isabelle Francais

recurrent seizures caused by a disturbance of brain function.

The seizure occurs suddenly and lasts about one minute, and the dog recovers spontaneously. The dog loses conscious-ness, his limbs and trunk stiffen, and he falls over on his side with severe rigidity of the muscles alternating with vigorous running motions. This usually will be accompanied by biting motions and salivation.

Recovery is complete but sometimes there may be a period of disorientation before complete recovery. There are variations to seizures, but most owners will realize that their dog is having a seizure by the second occurrence.

At this time, the cause of seizures, the reasons for them, and which dogs will have seizures are still being studied. If you feel your dog is subject to seizures, you should take him to the veterinarian. He will prescribe an anticonvulsant drug, and the condition will be kept under control. Seizures are a common problem in dogs and many can live a normal life with the anticonvulsant drug. There is no evidence that seizures are painful to a dog and often the owner is much more upset watching the disturbing event than is the dog that is unaware of what is happening.

CANCER

Cancer diagnosis can happen in any breed of dog, and Scotties are no exception. As in man, there is not always a cure, and again as in man, early detection is your best form of prevention. Check your dog over each time

THE GUIDE TO OWNING A SCOTTISH TERRIER

Dogs can pick up diseases from other dogs, so be sure to limit your puppy's human and canine visitors until he's had all of his vaccinations. *Photo: Isabelle Francais*

you groom him for any lumps or bumps that you have not noticed before. Fast-growing lumps are cause for concern, particularly when found around the mammary glands. Any lump that you do not like the look of or is growing rapidly should be checked by your veterinarian.

VACCINATIONS

Every Scottish terrier puppy should be vaccinated against the major canine diseases. These are distemper, leptospirosis, hepatitis, and canine parvovirus. Your puppy may have received a temporary vaccination against distemper before you purchased him, but ask the breeder to be sure.

The age at which vaccinations are given can vary, but will usually be when the pup is 8 to 12 weeks old. By this time, any protection given to the pup by antibodies received from his mother via her initial milk feeds will be losing their strength.

The puppy's immune system works on the basis that the white blood cells engulf and render harmless attacking bacteria. However, they must first recognize a potential enemy.

Vaccines are either dead bacteria or they are live, but in very small doses. Either type prompts the pup's defense system to attack them. When a large attack then comes (if it does), the immune system recognizes it and massive numbers of lymphocytes (white blood corpuscles) are mobilized to counter the attack. However, the ability of the cells to recognize these dangerous viruses can diminish over a period of time. It is therefore useful to provide annual reminders about the nature of the enemy. This is done by means of booster injections that keep the immune system on its alert. Immunization is not 100 percent guaranteed successful, but is very close to this. Certainly it is better than giving the puppy no protection.

Dogs are subject to other viral attacks, and if these are of a high-risk factor in your area, then your vet will suggest you have the puppy vaccinated against these as well.

Your puppy or dog should also be vaccinated against the deadly rabies virus. In fact, in many places it is illegal for your dog not to be vaccinated. This is to protect your dog, your family, and the rest of the animal population from this deadly virus that infects the nervous system and causes dementia and death.

Dogs, like all other animals, are capable of contracting problems and diseases that, if listed, would seem overwhelming. However,

Dogs can develop Lyme disease from ticks that are found in trees, brush, and high grasses. If you live in a high-risk area, make sure your Scottie is properly vaccinated. *Photo: Isabelle Francais*

It is important that the veterinarian you choose is familiar with the Scottish Terrier and is aware of any problems that the breed may experience. *Photo: Isabelle Francais*

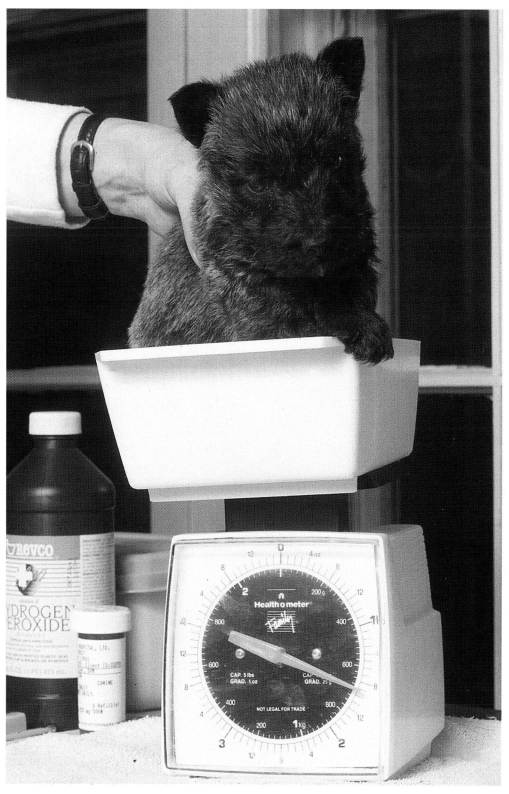

Good care from the very beginning can help to ensure that your Scottish Terrier puppy enjoys a healthy life. *Photo: Isabelle Francais*

in most cases these are easily avoided by sound husbandry—meaning well-bred and well-cared-for animals are less prone to developing diseases and problems than are carelessly bred and neglected animals. Your knowledge of how to avoid problems is far more valuable than all of the books and advice on how to cure them. Respectively, the only person you should listen to about treatment is your vet. Veterinarians don't have all the answers, but at least they are trained to analyze and treat illnesses and are aware of the full implications of treatments, which most others are not. This does not mean a few old remedies aren't good standbys when all else fails, but in most cases modern science provides the best treatments for disease.

PHYSICAL EXAMS

Your puppy should receive regular physical examinations or checkups. These come in two forms. One is obviously performed by your vet, and the other is a day-to-day procedure that should be done by you. Apart from the fact that the exam will highlight any problem at an early stage, it is an excellent way of socializing the pup to being handled.

To do the physical exam yourself, start at the head and work your way around the body. You are looking for any sign of lesions, or any indication of parasites on the pup. The most common parasites are fleas and ticks.

FIGHTING FLEAS

Fleas are very mobile and may be red, black, or brown in color. The adults suck the blood of the host, while the larvae feed on the feces of the adults, which is rich in blood. Flea "dirt" may be seen on the pup as very tiny clusters of blackish specks that look like freshly ground pepper. The eggs of fleas may be laid on the puppy, though they are more commonly laid off the host in a favorable place, such as the bedding. They normally hatch in 4 to 21 days, depending on the temperature, but they can survive for up to 18 months if temperature conditions are not favorable. The larvae are maggot-like and molt a couple of times before forming a pupae, which can survive long periods until the temperature, or the vibration of a nearby host, causes them to emerge and jump on the host.

There are a number of effective treatments available, and you should discuss them with your veterinarian, then follow all instructions for the one you choose. Any treatment will involve a product for your puppy or dog and one for the environment, and will require diligence on your part to treat all areas and thoroughly clean your home and yard until the infestation is eradicated.

THE TROUBLE WITH TICKS

Ticks are arthropods of the spider family, which means they have eight legs (though the larvae have six). They bury their headparts into the host and gorge on its blood. They are easily seen as small grain-like creatures sticking out from the skin. They are often picked up when dogs play in fields, but may also arrive in your yard via wild animals—even birds—or stray cats and dogs. Some ticks are species-specific, others are more adaptable and will host on many species.

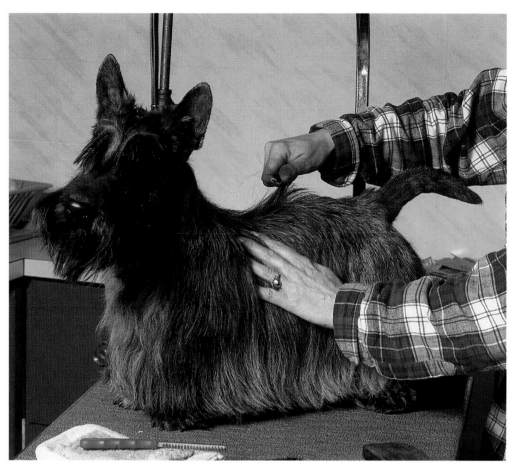

Check your Scottie's coat on a regular basis for any sign of external parasites, especially after he's been playing outside. *Photo: Isabelle Francais*

The most troublesome type of tick is the deer tick, which spreads the deadly Lyme disease that can cripple a dog (or a person). Deer ticks are tiny and very hard to detect. Often, by the time they're big enough to notice, they've been feeding on the dog for a few days—long enough to do their damage. Lyme disease was named for the area of the United States in which it was first detected—Lyme, Connecticut—but has now been diagnosed in almost all parts of the US. Your veterinarian can advise you of the danger to your dog(s) in your area, and may suggest your dog be vaccinated for Lyme. Always go over your dog with a fine-toothed flea comb when you come in from walking through any area that may harbor deer ticks, and if your dog is acting unusually sluggish or sore, seek veterinary advice.

Attempts to pull a tick free will invariably leave the headpart in the pup, where it will die and cause an infected wound or abscess. The best way to remove ticks is to dab a strong saline solution on them, or iodine, or alcohol. This will numb them, causing them to loosen their hold, at which time they can be removed with forceps. The wound can then be cleaned and covered with an antiseptic ointment. If ticks are common in your area, consult with your vet for a suitable

As a responsible Scottish Terrier owner, you should have a basic understanding of the medical problems that affect the breed.
Photo: Isabelle Francais

pesticide to be used in kennels, on bedding, and on the puppy or dog.

INSECTS AND OTHER OUTDOOR DANGERS

There are many biting insects, such as mosquitoes, that can cause discomfort to a puppy. Many diseases are transmitted by the males of these species. A pup can easily get a grass seed or thorn lodged between his pads or in the folds of his ears. These may go unnoticed until an abscess forms.

This is where your daily check of the puppy or dog will do a world of good. If your puppy has been playing in long grass or places where there may be thorns, pine needles, wild animals, or parasites, the checkup is a wise precaution.

SKIN DISORDERS

Apart from problems associated with lesions created by biting pests, a puppy may fall foul to a number of other skin disorders. Examples are ringworm, mange, and eczema. Ringworm is not caused by a worm, but is a fungal infection. It manifests itself as a sore-looking bald circle. If your puppy should have any form of bald patches on himself, let your veterinarian check him over; a microscopic examination can confirm the condition. Many old remedies for ringworm exist, such as iodine, carbolic acid, formalin, and other tinctures, but modern drugs are superior.

Fungal infections can be very difficult to treat, and even more difficult to eradicate, because of the spores. These can withstand most treatments, other than burning, which is the best thing to do with bedding once the condition has been confirmed.

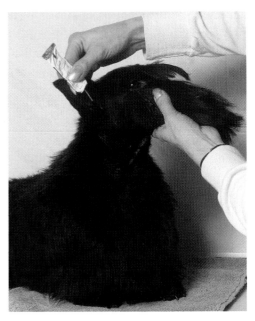

Your Scottie's ears need to be examined regularly and kept clean and free of dirt or buildup.
Photo: Isabelle Francais

Mange is a general term that can be applied to many skin conditions where the hair falls out and a flaky crust develops and falls away. Often, dogs will scratch themselves, and this invariably is worse than the original condition, for it opens lesions that are then subject to viral, fungal, or parasitic attack. The cause of the problem can be various species of mites. These either live on skin debris and the hair follicles, which they destroy, or they bury themselves just beneath the skin and feed on the tissue. Applying general remedies from pet stores is not recommended because it is essential to identify the type of mange before a specific treatment is effective.

Eczema is another nonspecific term applied to many skin disorders. The condition can be brought about in many ways. Sunburn, chemicals, allergies to foods, drugs, pollens—even stress—can all produce a deterioration of the skin and coat. Given the range of causal factors, treatment can be difficult because the problem is one of identification. It is a case of taking each possibility at a time and trying to correctly diagnose the matter. If the cause is of a dietary nature then you must remove one item at a time in order to find out if the dog is allergic to a given food. It could, of course, be the lack of a nutrient that is the problem, so if the condition persists, you should consult your veterinarian.

INTERNAL DISORDERS
It cannot be overstressed that it is very

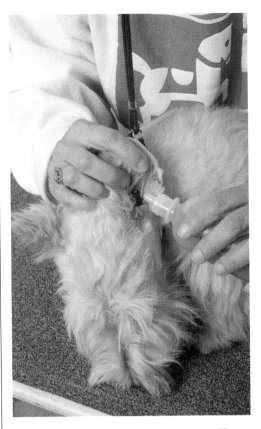

Routine ear cleaning will help ward off any infections or mite infestations in your Scottish Terrier. *Photo: Isabelle Francais*

foolish to attempt to diagnose an internal disorder without the advice of a veterinarian. Take a relatively common problem such as diarrhea. It might be caused by nothing more serious than the puppy hogging a lot of food or eating something that he has never previously eaten. Conversely, it could be the first indication of a potentially fatal disease. It's up to your veterinarian to make the correct diagnosis.

The following symptoms, especially if they accompany each other or are progressively added to earlier symptoms, mean you should visit the veterinarian right away:

Continual Vomiting

All dogs vomit from time to time and this is not necessarily a sign of illness. They will eat grass to induce vomiting. It is a natural cleansing process common to many carnivores. However, continued vomiting is a clear sign of a problem. It may be a blockage in the pup's intestinal tract, it may be induced by worms, or it could be due to any number of diseases.

Diarrhea

This, too, may be nothing more than a temporary condition due to many factors. Even a change of home can induce diarrhea, because this often stresses the pup, and invariably there is some change in the diet. If it persists more than 48 hours then something is amiss. If blood is seen in the feces, waste no time at all in taking the dog to the vet.

Running Eyes and/or Nose

A pup might have a chill and this will cause the eyes and nose to weep. Again, this should quickly clear up if the puppy is placed in a warm environment and away from any drafts. If it does not, and especially if a mucous discharge is seen, then the pup has an illness that must be diagnosed.

Wheezing or Coughing

Prolonged coughing is a sign of a problem, usually of a respiratory nature. If the pup

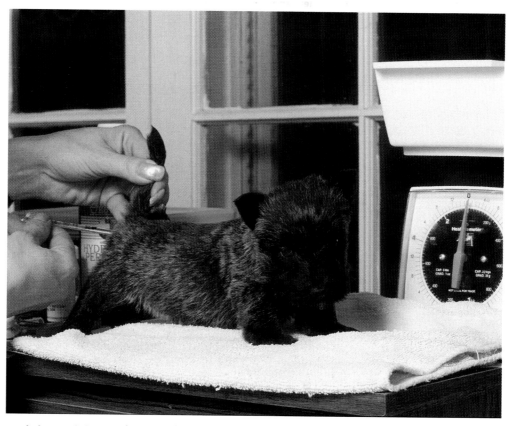

Any behavioral changes, temperature changes, or listlessness may indicate that your puppy is feeling ill. Take him to the veterinarian if you notice any of these symptoms. *Photo: Isabelle Francais*

THE GUIDE TO OWNING A SCOTTISH TERRIER

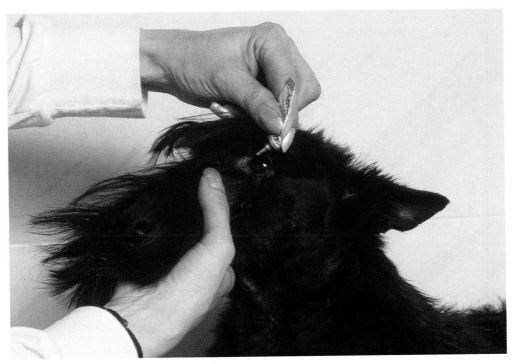

Your Scottish Terrier's eyes should be clear and free from any redness or irritation.
Photo: Isabelle Francais

has difficulty breathing and makes a wheezing sound when breathing, then something is wrong.

Cries When Eliminating
This might only be a minor problem due to the hard state of the feces, but it could be more serious, especially if the pup cries when urinating.

Cries When Touched
Obviously, if you do not handle a puppy with care he might yelp. However, if he cries even when lifted gently, then he has an internal problem that becomes apparent when pressure is applied to a given area of the body. Clearly, this must be diagnosed.

Refuses Food
Generally, puppies and dogs are greedy creatures when it comes to feeding time. Some might be fussier, but none should refuse more than one meal. If they go for a number of hours without showing any interest in their food, then something is not as it should be.

General Listlessness
All puppies have their off days when they do not seem their usual cheeky, mischievous selves. If this condition persists for more than two days then there is little doubt of a problem. They may not show any of the signs listed, other than perhaps a reduced interest in their food. There are many diseases that can develop internally without displaying obvious clinical signs. Blood, fecal, and other tests are needed in order to identify the disorder before it reaches an advanced state that may not be treatable.

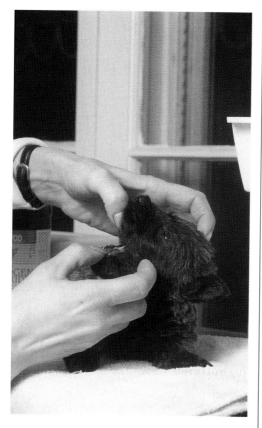

The Scottish Terrier is generally a healthy breed, and if loved and well cared for, will live a long and productive life. *Photo: Isabelle Francais*

WORMS

There are many species of worms, and a number of these live in the tissues of dogs and most other animals. Many create no problem at all, so you are not even aware they exist. Others can be tolerated in small levels, but become a major problem if they number more than a few. The most common types seen in dogs are roundworms and tapeworms. While roundworms are the greater problem, tapeworms require an intermediate host so are more easily eradicated.

Roundworms of the species *Toxocara canis* infest the dog. They may grow to a length of 8 inches (20 cm) and look like strings of spaghetti. The worms feed on the digesting food in the pup's intestines. In chronic cases the puppy will become pot-bellied, have diarrhea, and will vomit. Eventually, he will stop eating, having passed through the stage when he always seems hungry. The worms lay eggs in the puppy and these pass out in his feces. They are then either ingested by the pup, or they are eaten by mice, rats, or beetles. These may then be eaten by the puppy and the life cycle is complete.

Larval worms can migrate to the womb of a pregnant bitch or to her mammary glands, and this is how they pass to the puppy. The pregnant bitch can be wormed, which will help. The pups can, and should, be wormed when they are about two weeks old. Repeat worming every 10 to 14 days and the parasites should be removed. Worms can be extremely dangerous to young puppies, so you should be sure the pup is wormed as a matter of routine.

Tapeworms can be seen as tiny rice-like eggs sticking to the puppy's or dog's anus. They are less destructive, but still undesirable. The eggs are eaten by mice, fleas, rabbits, and other animals that serve as intermediate hosts. They develop into a larval stage and the host must be eaten by the dog in order to complete the chain. Your vet will supply a suitable remedy if tapeworms are seen or suspected. The vet can also do an egg count on the pup's feces under the microscope; this will indicate the extent of an infestation.

There are other worms, such as hookworms and whipworms, that are also blood suckers. They will make a pup anemic, and blood might be seen in the feces, which can be examined by the vet to confirm their presence. Cleanliness in all matters is the best preventative measure for all worms.

BLOAT (GASTRIC DILATATION)

This condition has proved fatal in many dogs, especially large and deep-chested breeds, such as the Rottweiler or the Great Dane. However, any dog can get bloat. It is caused by gases building up in the stomach, especially in the small intestine. What happens is that carbohydrates are fermented and release gases. Normally, these gases are released by belching or by being passed from the anus. If for any reason these exits become blocked (such as if the stomach twists due to physical exertion), the gases cannot escape and the stomach simply swells and places pressure on other organs, sometimes cutting off the blood supply to the heart or causing suffocation. Death can easily follow if the condition goes undetected.

The best preventative measure is not to feed large meals or exercise your puppy or dog immediately after he has eaten. You can reduce the risk of flatulence by feeding more fiber in the diet, not feeding too many dry biscuits, and possibly by adding activated charcoal tablets to the diet.

ACCIDENTS

All puppies will get their share of bumps and bruises due to the rather energetic way they play. These will usually rectify themselves over a few days. Small cuts should be bathed with a suitable disinfectant and then smeared with an antiseptic ointment. If a cut looks more serious, then stem the flow of blood with a towel or makeshift tourniquet and rush the pup to the veterinarian. Never apply so much pressure to the wound that it might restrict the flow of blood to the limb.

In the case of burns, you should apply cold water or an ice pack to the surface. If the burn was due to a chemical then this must be washed away with copious amounts of water. Trim away the hair if need be. Wrap the dog in a blanket and rush him to the vet. The pup may go into shock, depending on the severity of the burn, and this will result in a lowered blood pressure,

All Scotties will get their share of bumps and bruises in the course of growing up, but if your dog sustains a serious injury, it is best to take him to the veterinarian immediately.
Photo: Isabelle Francais

As your dog matures, his energy level may drop and he may need more assistance in his daily activities. Help him to adjust and make him as comfortable as possible. *Photo: Isabelle Francais*

which is dangerous and the reason the pup must receive immediate veterinary attention.

If a broken limb is suspected then try to keep the animal as still as possible. Wrap your pup or dog in a blanket to restrict movement and get him to the veterinarian as soon as possible. Do not move the dog's head so it is tilting backward, as this might result in blood entering the lungs.

Do not let your pup jump up and down from heights, as this can cause considerable shock to the joints. Like all youngsters, puppies do not know when enough is enough, so you must do all their thinking for them.

Provided you apply strict hygiene to all aspects of your puppy's husbandry, and you make daily checks on his physical state, you have done as much as you can to safeguard him during his most vulnerable period. Routine visits to your veterinarian are also recommended, especially while the puppy is under one year of age. The vet may notice something that did not seem important to you.

THE GERIATRIC DOG

The geriatric dog (a dog over eight years of age) may require a little more or different care than the younger dog. As your dog ages, he will slow down and possibly have some arthritis. His sight and hearing may start waning, and he may sleep more. Let him have his way. Do not expect him to do the three-mile walk he did as a pup. You may want to try dog food for the geriatric or sedate dog. Be sure he has a warm space to sleep and try to keep him at a normal weight, as excess weight can be difficult on the rheumatoid bones.

As he ages and becomes more infirm, you will eventually be confronted with the decision of putting your dog down. Unfortunately, dogs and humans do not die very often in their sleep. With the dog, though, we are able to make the decision to be a humane owner and the day may come when you take your pet in to be euthanized by your veterinarian. It's hard to know when "it's time" but again, use your common sense and try not to let the dog suffer unduly. Your veterinarian will administer a very quick drug and you will be surprised as to how quickly and peacefully he will die in your arms. This is a terribly sad day for the entire family, but it often takes only a few weeks or months before you are off looking for your new Scottish Terrier.

There is no limit to the mischief that a young Scottie puppy can make. By supervising him closely and performing daily health checks, you can ensure his safety and well-being. *Photo: Isabelle Francais*

Index